em.bold.en

1. give (someone) the courage or
confidence to do something or
behave in a certain way.

Embolden

Published By Arabelle Publishing
PO Box 2841
Chesterfield, VA 23832

Credits:
Foreword written by Sasha Sillcut
Cover and Interior Design Julie Basinski
Editing Clara Rose with Intentional Influence

Library of Congress control number 2021932570
Subjects Mind & Body / Spirituality / Self Help
Paperback ISBN 9781735632827

Printed in the United States of America, 2021

Group Sales:
Books are available in special quantity discounts when purchased directly from the publisher in bulk by corporations, organizations, and special interest groups. For more information, please email the publisher at hello@arabellepublishing.com

Embolden

Brave Steps to Help You Conquer Fears and Insecurities

amy and blair
debrucque

Arabelle Publishing, LLC
Chesterfield, VA

foreword

I met Amy Debrucque when I was a guest on her podcast, Life on Purpose. We hit it off immediately, as we shared several similar interests: empowering and encouraging women to find their "brave", sharing an authentic voice in an Instagram-perfect world, and laughing over parenting challenges. The more I spent time with Amy, the greater depth of respect I had for her. It takes immense fortitude to be positive and uplifting despite suffering some of life's greatest loss, and Amy has it.

Amy's experiences of overcoming debilitating anxiety set a strong foundation for Embolden. Throughout the book, Amy provides a much-needed script to face your fears head on. Her words of stepping forward are much needed in our world today, where anxiety, doubt and stress percolate. Amy's expertise on rising above anxiety and limiting beliefs is what makes her the perfect person to write Embolden. Through Embolden, Amy shares with young women how to embrace their faith to overcome their worries and grow.

As an author, I know the most meaningful books are those written where the topic is close to the heart. Readers will find that with Embolden, Amy has poured her passion, strength, and soul into every page. Amy's clear direction, sage advice, and authentic wisdom makes Embolden the perfect gift to encourage young women to find their way in a worry-ridden world.

Dr. Sasha Shillcutt

Physician, Founder, and Author of *Between Grit and Grace*

dedication

to Caren

Thank you for your Godly influence and being
the best role model any sister could ask for.

Watching you raise your incredible daughters,
encouraged and reminded us of the importance
and impact our faith can make in young women's lives.

table of contents

acknowledgments

A heartfelt thank you to Blair for giving me this once in a lifetime opportunity to work side by side with not only my daughter but also a woman I admire.

To my family and friends who have loved and supported me throughout this writing journey despite my introverted ways, Andy, Karen, Alice, Sues, Deb A., Deb O., Kim, MJ, Rachael, and Nicolle, I love you. Your encouragement has been unwavering and has given me the confidence to chase this crazy dream.

A special thank you to Clara for reminding me to breathe, keeping me focused, and editing my words so people will want to read them.

To all my children, you will always be my greatest accomplishments. Sam, you inspire me to be brave every day by serving this country. Ethan, your compassion for others is something I aspire to. To Adeline, aka Patty Cake, your love and loyalty to your family and friends fill my heart.

To my parents, who are my biggest cheerleaders, I love you for all you are and do for my family and me.

Last, but most important to Ron, who is the most courageous person I know. Thank you for patiently allowing me to see this writing dream come true by always believing in me, getting me out of my comfort zone, and showing me that being brave is easier with you by my side.

acknowledgments

I want to give a special thank you to my Mom for the opportunity to create this journal with her; it means so much to be part of your writing journey.

To Claire Senerman and Rachel Rennie, thank you for being such incredible role models. I don't have older sisters, so I have always looked up to both of you, and I'm very lucky that I've had such strong Christian women to follow.

To my little sister Addy, I wanted to create something that would help you as you got older, so thank you for inspiring me to make this journal, and I hope it will bring encouragement to you and other young women.

blair

Embolden

Take a seat and grab your favorite drink.

This book was designed specifically for you. This is an exciting time to be encouraged for the beautiful life God has prepared for you.

Use it anyway you want. Journal, highlight, take notes, or just read the inspirations.

However you use it, we pray that it leaves you feeling confident, brave and bold in this next step of life.

Emboldening ourselves helps to embolden others.

God Bless

amy and blair

Let's be women who lift
and empower each other.

this book is for:

_____

Life is a journey...

All you need is
direction to find
your true destination.

week one...
fearless

PERFECT
LOVE
DRIVES
OUT
FEAR

day one: *be brave*

Sometimes when we're scared, it's hard to remember to give it up to **God** instead of handling it ourselves.

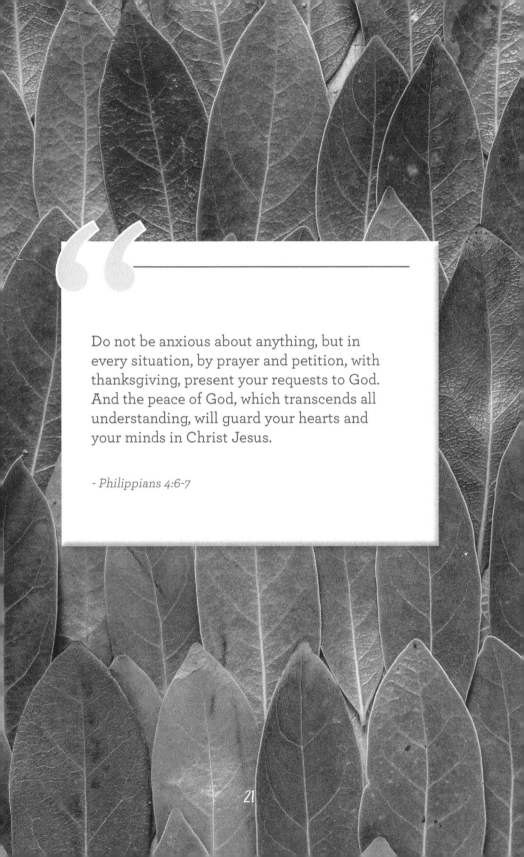

"

―――――――――――――――――――

Do not be anxious about anything, but in every situation, by prayer and petition, with thanksgiving, present your requests to God. And the peace of God, which transcends all understanding, will guard your hearts and your minds in Christ Jesus.

- *Philippians 4:6-7*

identify your fears

What fears are holding you back?

Jot down things that keep you up at night or make
you anxious throughout the day. Expose your fears,
surrender them to God, and eliminate their power over you.

_____

_____

_____

_____

_____

_____

_____

_____

_____

_____

_____

_____

_____

_____

_____

_____

_____

day two: *start small*

Do one thing today that you've been afraid of doing.
Write it down here and describe how it made you feel.

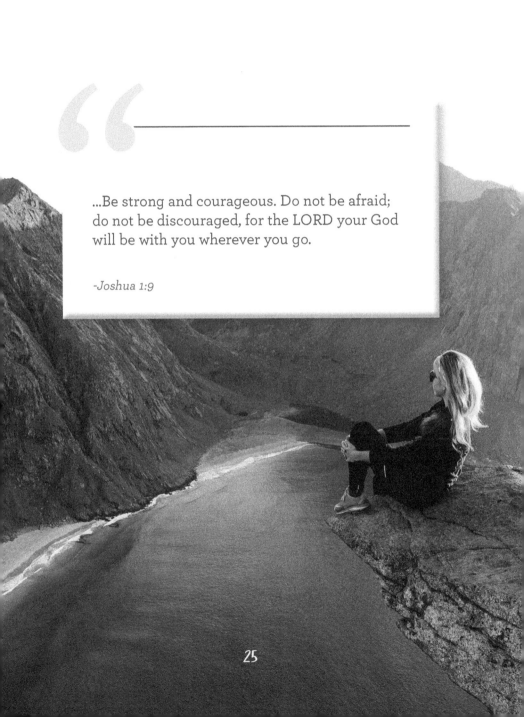

> ...Be strong and courageous. Do not be afraid; do not be discouraged, for the LORD your God will be with you wherever you go.
>
> *-Joshua 1:9*

week 1

"

Fear is normal,
but courage gets
the final say...

day three: *pause*

and take a deep breath...

The Lord replied,
"My Presence will
go with you, and
I will give you rest."

-Exodus 33:14

30

take a calming *breath*

Easy breathing technique

1. Put your finger on your right nostril and breathe in through your nose slowly.

2. Switch your finger to your left nostril and breath out slowly.

3. Repeat until you feel relaxed, then take three deep breaths, breathing in and out with both nostrils.

day four: *courage*

is the opposite of fear...
Sometimes we have to go out of our
comfort zone to gain independence
and dispel our fears.

keep it
simple

34

in the comfort *zone*

What are some ways you can get
out of your comfort zone today?
(mark all that apply)

- Talk to someone new

- Join a club at school

- Explore outside of your safe zone

- Do something alone

- Do something with new people

- Take a fitness class that would
  normally intimidate you

day five: *a note from* blair

I am an introverted person, so getting out of my comfort zone can be a challenge. I would rather just stick to my normal routine and things I'm comfortable with. But I found that to grow as a person it's important to go out of your comfort zone. It took me a while to force myself to do this, and at first it gave me a lot of anxiety and made me really nervous. But little by little it got easier to do, and now even though it still intimidates me at first, I know it will benefit me in the future.

"
_____

be strong
&
courageous

-Joshua 1:9

day six: memorize

Philippians 4:16
John 4:18
Isaiah 35:4
Isaiah 40:31

Scriptures

helpful resources

Daily inspiration app

 first 5

Anxiety reducing apps

 calm   breathwrk   dare

first5.org and healthline.com (search "best anxiety apps")

41

day seven: a day of rest

"Come to me...and I will give you rest." Matthew 11:28

a face mask to *relax*

a simple and soothing mask made with
banana, plain yogurt and honey

1. Peel the banana and cut in half. Put half
   in a mixing bowl and mash until it's creamy.

2. Add 2 Tablespoons of the yogurt to the
   mashed banana and blend well.

3. Pour 1 Tablespoon of honey into the banana
   yogurt mixture. Blend well.

4. Apply the mixture to your face evenly.
   Avoid getting it in your eyes.

5. Leave on for 15-20 minutes and rinse with
   cool water and pat dry.

Pro tips
- Use it once or twice per week to keep your skin looking healthy.
- Only use ripe bananas; green ones won't mash!
- Make sure the yogurt is mixed well before adding it to the banana.
- Use raw honey that has no additives.

week two...
kindness

SMALL

THINGS

SHOW

GREAT

LOVE

day one: *kindness is simple*

A warm hello.
Listening.
Encouraging a friend.
Withholding judgment.

> Be kind and compassionate
> to one another, forgiving each
> other, just as in Christ, God
> forgave you.
>
> *- Ephesians 4:32*

kindness is:

the quality of being friendly,
generous, and considerate.

sometimes fear
can hinder us

Sometimes our fears can hinder us from
expressing small acts of kindness.
What are some of those fears?

Rejection?   Embarrassment?

Peers?   Image?

day two: *start small*

Do one act of kindness today
that you normally wouldn't.

Note it here, and how you felt about it.

_____

_____

_____

_____

_____

_____

_____

_____

_____

_____

_____

_____

> Therefore, as God's chosen people, holy and dearly loved, clothe yourselves with compassion, kindness, humility, gentleness, and patience.
>
> *~ Colossians 3:12*

KINDNESS
SPOTLIGHTS
THE BEAUTY
THAT CAN
COME FROM
UNEXPECTED
PLACES.

day three: *grace is a skill*

Perfecting it takes practice.

practice Tips

Ways to get started

- Put yourself in someone else's shoes.

- Try looking at another's view on something you're struggling to understand.

- Understanding someone else's view doesn't require you to change yours.

GRACE STREET COFFEE

"

Kindness is a language which
the deaf can hear and the blind can see.

— *Mark Twain*

KINDNESS

IS

AN

EXPRESSION

OF

GRACE

day four: *describe today*

Who are you?

Mark the words that describe you TODAY.

---

spirited

kind

stubborn

defiant

dependent

friendly

fulfilled

lost

searching

hopeful

TODAY
I AM
GRATEFUL 60

change your _mindset_

For 30 days acknowledge three
things you are grateful for. Speak
those affirmations daily to begin
a new habit of gratitude.

This practice will help you focus on the positive things
in your life and you'll be more apt to extend that same
positivity and kindness to others.

day five: *a note from* amy

Sometimes it feels easier to keep to ourselves and not reach out to others. However, God encourages us to do the opposite. What we put out to others is contagious. So, if we want to live in a world with compassion for others, WE must show compassion first.

make
people
feel
loved
today

"

Kind words can be short and easy to speak, but their echos are truly endless.

— *Mother Teresa*

What kind words can you speak today?

day six: *kindness & grace*

"She opens her mouth with wisdom, and the teaching of kindness is on her tongue."
Proverbs 31:26 (ESV)

helpful resources

Learning to practice grace
Practicinggrace.net

25 ways to be kind
doyouyoga.com/25-ways-tobekind-88843/

day seven: *bake something*

Eat in sweats with vanilla ice cream,
alone or with a friend.
Either way eat in sweats! Yum!

how to make an
easy galette

ingredients

- pre-made pie crust (rolled out)
- your favorite fruit
- 1/4 cup sugar
- 1/2 teaspoon cinnamon (optional)
- 1/2 squeezed lemon (optional)
- dusting of powdered sugar (optional)
- Egg-wash: for a golden brown crust.
  beat one egg. Add 2 T milk or water and
  brush on top crust. Sprinkle with sugar.

---

combine
In a small bowl combine berries, sugar
and cinnamon, and lemon juice.

fill
Fill the center of the pie crust and
fold in the sides.

brush
Brush edges with milk or eggwash
and sprinkle with sugar.

bake
350 degrees for 30 min.

week three...
temptations

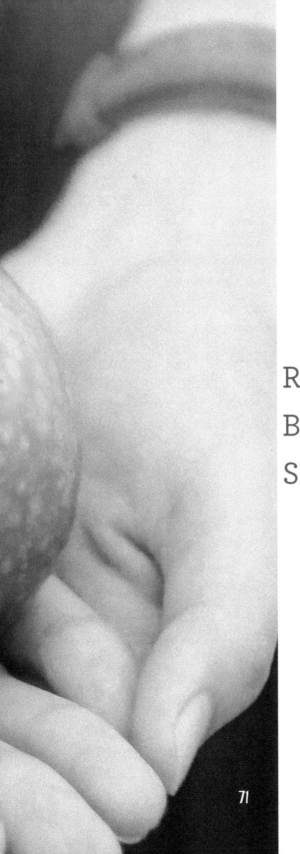

RESISTANCE
BRINGS
STRENGTH

day one: *identify*

your temptations: as your first step to
overcome them, keep your eyes wide open.

resisting can be *hard*

- A bad behavior or attitude

- Interrupting

- Judging

- Refusing good advice

- Other_____

avoid temptations

Practice new, healthy behaviors daily,
ditch the old, unhealthy ones.

Here are a few ways to help keep your
mind and heart in the right place.

_____

pray   Asking for God's guidance every day help's
reign in our desires to act without thinking.

replace   In the space you would normally fill a
negative temptation, do a positive action.

repeat   The more you do and don't do something
unhealthy the more it becomes habit.

day two: *gossiping*

Has gossip been something you've taken part in or been on the receiving end of?

How did it make you feel?

When contemplating sharing someone else's words remember, unless it happened to you, it's not your story to tell.

Do not let any unwholesome talk come out of your mouths, but only what is helpful for building others up according to their needs, that it may benefit those who listen.

- Ephesians 4:29

day three: *harmless or harmful?*

Spending too much time on superficial
stuff can hinder our personal growth.

Write down what temptations might be
separating you from better things.

---

hidden temptations

Re-evaluate the list below and decide if they've
become less casual and more obsessions.

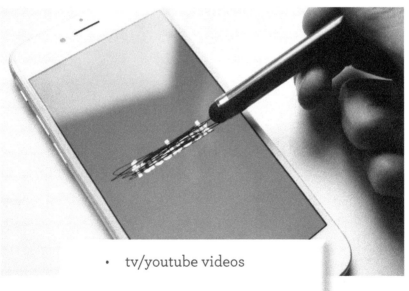

- tv/youtube videos

- social media
- checking your phone

- going out too much

Love is patient.
Love is kind.
It does not envy
or boast.
It is not proud,
rude, or self-seeking.
It is not easily angry
and keeps no record
of past mistakes.
It does not delight
in evil.
It rejoices in the tur
turuth.

82

"IF YOU
JUDGE
PEOPLE YOU
HAVE NO
TIME
TO LOVE
THEM."

-Mother Teresa

day four: *sharpen*

You don't have to struggle with the same temptation to help someone else with theirs.

Find an accountability partner that can offer and receive support.

> As iron sharpens iron so one person sharpens another.
>
> - *Proverbs 27:17*

think *about*

how might life be different, or even better
for you without these temptations...

Because he himself suffered when he was tempted, he is able to help those who are being tempted.

- Hebrews 2:18

day five: *pray and listen*

Make sure you're listening
for God's voice above all others.

> Watch and pray so that you will not fall into temptation. The spirit is willing, but the flesh is weak.
>
> -Matthew 26:41

AND LEAD
US NOT
INTO
TEMPTATION,
BUT DELIVER
US FROM
THE EVIL ONE.

- Mathew 6:13

day six: *a note from* blair

For me, the biggest way I resist temptation is by prevention. I try to remove things out of my life that would put me in a situation where I would be tempted with something I know I shouldn't do. It can be hard to do depending on what it is, but I try to remember that I am removing it for a purpose, and it will ultimately benefit me in the long run.

94

week 3

day seven: *carry it with you*

It's easier to remember God's Words when
they are right next to you.

make your own mini *Bible*

buy   Buy a small notebook

look up   Look up verses that offer encouragement in times of temptation.

jot down   Jot verses down in notebook.

keep   Keep in a purse, backpack, or bedside table.

Pro tip
- Use verses in this book to get started.

week four

growth

BLOOM
WHERE
YOU ARE
PLANTED

day one: *God has the power*

to bloom something ordinary into
something extraordinary.

you are
extraordinary.

growing is  *Trying*

taking yourself from yesterday
and trying to be better for today.

where do you see yourself *growing?*

Think of the places you need the most personal growth.

Knowing where you want to grow helps you become intentional about finding ways to make it happen.

day two: *identify*

Identify your strengths & weaknesses.

Acknowledge where you're at today so you can determine your starting point for tomorrow.

Where are you the strongest and the weakest? Write it here.

_____

_____

_____

_____

_____

_____

_____

_____

_____

_____

knowing

is growing

setting your
goals

The Good & Bad: list them

Use the questions below to acknowledge
your strengths and address your weaknesses.

The
good

What am I good at?

What have others noticed I do well?

Where do I thrive?

What motivates me?

What excites me?

Do I put in 100% effort?

Where can I add value to my life?

The
bad

What drains me?

What do I avoid doing?

What do I dislike?

What could I be doing more of?

What turns me off?

What turns others off about me?

Do my values align with my actions?

ways to *grow*

own it
Own your own junk - if you make a mistake, say so.

apologize
A simple I'm sorry, speaks volumes about the kind of person you are, or want to become.

forgive
Unless you're perfect, be willing to forgive others for their mistakes. You don't have to receive grace, in order to give it.

Be the bigger person.

day three: *let's get personal*

Who do you want to be today, tomorrow, and in the future?
Jot down your thoughts, and be honest, this is all about YOU.

Progress over perfection. I'm worth the effort, because God
says so!

> For nothing will be impossible with God.
>
> *-Luke 1:37 (ESV)*

BE MINDFUL WHERE
YOU LOOK FOR
GUIDANCE.
GOD'S WORDS
AND LOVE ARE
THE FOUNDATION
TO GROWTH.
IT IS THROUGH HIM,
WHERE WE FIND
OUR PURPOSE

> _____
>
> ...so that you may live a life worthy of the Lord and please him in every way: bearing fruit in every good work, growing in the knowledge of God...
>
> -Colossians 1:10

" _____

Be diligent in these matters; give yourself wholly to them, so that everyone may see your progress.

-1 Timothy 4:15

day four: *progress over perfection*

Don't abandon God's direction when things fall short.

Get back on your bike and try again.
The efforts to change and grow are more
important than the execution even if it stings a bit.

"

I planted the seed, Apollos watered it, but God has been making it grow. So neither the one who plants nor the one who waters is anything, but only God, who makes things grow. The one who plants and the one who waters have one purpose, and they will each be rewarded according to their own labor.

-1 Corinthians 3:6-8

day five: *resources for growth*

To keep you encouraged and focused, try memorizing
a simple scripture like: Romans 3:23

It's important to find relationships that foster growth.
Make sure you have a balance of "yes" friends with others
who are willing and brave enough to help bring out your
best even if you don't want to hear it.

Write a short list of who can help you be the best version
God created you to be.

_____

_____

_____

_____

_____

_____

_____

_____

_____

_____

"

For all have sinned and fall short
of the glory of God...

-Romans 3:23

day six: *reward yourself today*

celebrate a victory

treat *yourself*

splurge on a fancy coffee

buy a new pair of shoes

get a manicure

Be proud of yourself for making strides towards
living intentionally for a greater purpose.

day seven: *growth takes place*

the minute we decide to change for the better

How did you feel at the start of this journal?

Where is your heart and head resting now?

Is there more work to be done?

review and *rewind*

Only YOU will have the answers. Write them here.

small wins
are still wins

Acknowledge your wins.

Write them down from the beginning of this journey

BIG and small.

_____

_____

_____

_____

_____

_____

_____

_____

_____

_____

_____

_____

from amy and blair

resources

and letters

Thank you for the opportunity to share and encourage hope in your life. At almost 50 years old, I've learned that your age doesn't disqualify you from pain and struggles. At 26 years old, I experienced 2 devastating losses that would produce 15 years of anxiety and fear. Within those 15 years, I had to learn that every struggle is an opportunity to grow. Personal growth continues to move us forward towards the life and purpose God created for us.

Reflect, seek godly fellowship among your peers, and remember you're not alone in this life. Still, and most important, know that YOU are an amazing imperfect creation of an ALL loving God. God Bless.

what I am loving in faith and life *amy*

faith first5 app. + my journaling Bible, from
rusticjournals on etsy

health doTerra essential vitamins +
70% plantbased diet/30% all foods + 100%
chocolate

beauty doTerra skincare + NYX butter gloss +
primally pure deodorant

Trends modern rustic anything in black and white

home

life white rustic brick + throw pillows
shoes + classic blazer + rebounding
+ patent loafers + white tank

I hope this book encouraged you to conquer things that might have scared you before. I have struggled with letting my anxiety stop me from doing things the Lord was calling me to do, which is why I wanted to create this book. When I first went to college, I felt God calling me to a different career and educational path than I had set for myself. I resisted for a while because I was too scared to disappoint my parents or go into something new I hadn't just spent years preparing for. But once I finally listened to His calling, I saw how much better the career He laid out for me was. It's opened up so many great opportunities I wouldn't have had if I hadn't listened. So, I encourage you to follow God's plan for you and listen to his voice above all others, even if it's scary at first. He will guide you through it, and the end result will be so worth it. God Bless.

what I am loving in faith and life *blair*

faith
3 minute devotions for women +
the Bible study (old & new testament)

health
intermittent fasting 16:8 +
lots of herbal tea

beauty
belei vitamin C moisturizer +
glossier futuredew serum

Trends
coffee culture

home
hanging plant holders

life
mystery books (all books really) +
kickboxing

photo credits*
cover image by Drew Graham; Unsplash

Pg. 71 Photo by Jonathan Meyer

Pg. 73 Photo by Andrea Tummons

Pg. 74 Photo by Roberto Nickson

Pg. 75 Photo by Roberto Nickson

Pg. 76 Photo by Jr Korpa

Pg. 78 Photo by Romina veliz

Pg. 79 Photo by Romina veliz

Pg. 81 Photo by Alex Geerts

Pg. 82 Photo by Annie Spratt

Pg. 85 Photo by Rosie Kerr

Pg. 86 Photo by Stanislav Kondratiev

Pg. 89 Photo by Mustafa Omar

Pg. 90 Photo by Liana De Laurent

Pg. 93 Photo by Kalen Emsley

Pg. 94 Photo by Luca Bravo

Pg. 97 Photo by Helena Hertz

Pg. 99 Photo by Annie Spratt

Pg. 100 Photo by Brian Harris

Pg. 101 Photo by Matt Quinn

Pg. 102 Photo by Muzaffar Abasov

Pg. 105 My Image Watkins Glenn Gorge

Pg. 106 Photo by Brigitte Tohm

Pg. 108 Photo by My Life Journal

Pg. 111 Photo by Allef Vinicius

Pg. 112 Photo by Henri Pham

Pg. 114 Photo by Sylwia Forysinska

Pg. 116 Photo by Tyler Nix

Pg. 118 Blair Photo by Root & Wander
Photography

Pg. 120 Amy & Blair by Root & Wander
Photography

resource credits

Doterra skincare - doterra.com

Journaling bible - rusticjournals on etsy.com

*Photos courtesy of Unsplash, unless noted